Figure Locations and Descriptions Tulsa, Oklahoma

Figure 1: Black Wall Street on Fire

Figure 2: Black Wall Street Before the Fire

Figure 3: Aftermath of the Tulsa Fire

Native American Territory

Figure 4: Native American Family

Japanese Internment Camps

Figure 5: Japanese Internment Family

Southern United States

Figure 6: Sharecropper Family

U.S. Congress, Washington

Figure 7: Black Caucus 117th

Organize, Don't Criticize

"Organize and Empower Our Own: Overcome the Forces That Divide Us."

By Dr. Eldridge Henderson

Published by Amazon
Made in the USA
Columbia, SC
December 8, 2024

Copyright © 2024 Dr. Eldridge Henderson. All rights reserved. No part of this book may be reproduced, stored in a retrieval system, or transmitted in any form or by any means—electronic, mechanical, photocopying, recording, or otherwise—without prior written permission from the copyright owner, except for brief excerpts used in reviews or for educational purposes.

Preface

This book explores the deeply rooted and systemic challenges facing the Black community, particularly in politics, education, economics, and leadership. Through a lens sharpened by years of experience, I have aimed to present practical strategies and solutions that empower Black Americans to reclaim agency in shaping their future. This work reflects my life's commitment to social justice and community development. It seeks to provide readers with the knowledge of historical and current struggles and the tools to make meaningful change.

This is more than a book; it is a call to action. With eight critical years left to transform the political, social, and economic standing of Black Americans, it is imperative to rethink our approach, rebuild our communities, and challenge the systems that have long held us back. My goal is to inspire a new generation of leaders who will not only criticize but organize, who will demand justice and actively create it through coalition building, strategic voting, and self-empowerment.

I hope this book serves as a guide, sparking conversations and actions to bring about the systemic change needed for Black Americans to achieve true equality and prosperity.

Preface Addition: The Importance of Organizing Over Criticizing

In the pursuit of systemic change, it is essential to prioritize **organizing over criticizing**. *Criticism alone, while often necessary to identify the barriers and injustices we face, offers no direct pathway to meaningful solutions. Human enemies—whether oppressive systems, unjust policies, or discriminatory practices—should be met with awareness,* **coordinated action, and coalition-building**. *This book underscores the belief that transformation comes from community-driven strategies that inspire collective action.*

"Empowering individuals to organize rather than just critique is the cornerstone of progress."

Throughout this book, artificial intelligence contributes insights to deepen discussions at the end of each chapter. A.I.'s observations offer additional clarity, potential solutions, and a future-oriented perspective. This integration reflects the importance of leveraging modern tools and diverse perspectives in fighting for equality and justice. After each chapter, you will find AI-generated reflections encouraging readers to take tangible steps in line with the ideas presented. These reflections are designed to help focus actions, enhance understanding, and stimulate creative solutions for the challenges.

Contents

Figure Locations and Descriptions Tulsa, Oklahoma 1

Copyright 5

Preface 6

   Chapter 1: Education and Training 9

      Addressing Challenges and Solutions in Inner-City Communities: A Call to Action 9

   Chapter 2: Religion 15

      Nurturing Faith and Empowering Futures: A Holistic Approach to Family Development 15

   Chapter 3: Leadership 22

      Empowering Through Leadership: Creating Lasting Impact in Communities 22

   Chapter 4: Economic Development 29

   Faith and Financial Resilience: Building Prosperity Through Strategic Empowerment 29

   Chapter 5: Politics 35

      Leadership and Coalition Building: Paving the Way for Lasting Change 35

   Chapter 6: Corrective Action Plan for Global Solutions 42

      Implementing Strategic Steps to Unite, Innovate, and Drive Lasting Change. 42

   Appendix: 49

      5-Year Plan for Regional Resort Development 49

      Banking Establishment Plan: Regional Centers and Main Bank 61

Impact and Vision 68

   Acknowledgment of A.I. Contribution 70

   About the Author 71

Acknowledgments 72

What Readers Are Saying About "Organize, Don't Criticize" 73

Chapter 1: Education and Training

Addressing Challenges and Solutions in Inner-City Communities: A Call to Action

The fear of the Lord is the beginning of knowledge, but fools despise wisdom and instruction. (Proverbs 1:7 NIV)
Start children off on the way they should go, and even when they are old they will not turn from it. (Proverbs 22:6 NIV)

Introduction

> The surge in crime rates across American cities has raised urgent questions about public safety and the effectiveness of crime prevention policies. This chapter focuses on the significant challenges inner-city communities face, particularly the rise in crime, and highlights key factors contributing to this crisis. Moreover, it proposes a series of practical solutions to reduce crime and empower communities through education, economic development, and strong social engagement.

Identification of Problems

- Rising crime rates in inner-city communities
- Economic instability and lack of opportunities
- Gang affiliations among youth
- Limited access to quality education
- Insufficient vocational training programs
- Lack of mentorship and positive role models
- Persistent systemic racism

- Disparities in mental health resources
- Absence of community-driven initiatives
- Limited public engagement in crime prevention strategies

Identification of Solutions

- Strengthening education with mentorship programs and after-school tutoring
- Implementing vocational training programs and apprenticeship opportunities
- Developing entrepreneurship programs and financial literacy workshops
- Launching community centers for cultural and social relevance
- Encouraging youth engagement through extracurricular activities and leadership training
- Promoting economic empowerment through business incubators and micro-loan programs
- Establishing mental health resources and support groups within the community
- Organizing cultural festivals and events to celebrate heritage and promote unity
- Forming mentorship networks that connect younger and older generations
- Expanding safe spaces for emotional well-being and social-emotional skill development

Benefits

1. Empowered Youth: Access to quality education, mentorship, and vocational training programs will reduce gang affiliations and create paths to success, providing young people with opportunities for personal and professional growth.

2. Economic Stability: Entrepreneurship programs, financial literacy workshops, and business incubators will boost local economies, offering financial empowerment and reducing reliance on external resources.

3. Stronger Communities: Establishing community centers and organizing cultural events will foster unity, increase civic engagement, and strengthen social ties.

4. Mental Health and Well-being: Accessible mental health resources and emotional support groups will improve community members' well-being, helping them cope with the pressures of systemic challenges.

5. Crime Reduction: By addressing the root causes of crime through education, economic opportunities, and social engagement, the overall crime rate in inner-city communities can decrease, promoting safer neighborhoods.

Conclusion

> By implementing these solutions, inner-city communities can overcome challenges and create opportunities for growth and resilience. The benefits of education, economic empowerment, and emotional well-being are far-reaching, fostering empowered youth, economic stability, and stronger communities. The collective impact will lead to a safer, more unified environment where crime rates drop, and the future is filled with opportunity.

Call to Action

> Now is the time for action. We must unite to create change in these communities, ensuring that each of us plays a role in the transformation. Please refer to the feedback checklist below to assess your understanding of the issues. Achieving a score of 8 out of 10 signifies successful comprehension and readiness to respond to the challenges outlined.

Instructions: Use this checklist to track your progress by marking "Yes" or "No" responses on paper or in your digital notes.

Feedback Checklist

1. Identified the key problems in inner-city communities. Yes[] No[]
2. Recognized the role of economic instability. Yes[] No[]

3. I understand the importance of vocational training. Yes[] No[]
4. Addressed the need for mentorship and positive role models. Yes[] No[]
5. Acknowledged the systemic issues of racism and inequality. Yes[] No[]
6. Highlighted the value of mental health resources. Yes[] No[]
7. Recognize the importance of community-driven initiatives. Yes[] No[]
8. Understood the role of cultural and social relevance. Yes[] No[]
9. Identified safe spaces for emotional development. Yes[] No[]
10. Provided actionable solutions for crime prevention strategies. Yes[] No[]

Success Criteria: 8 out of 10 "Yes" responses = success.

A.I. Reflections and Suggested Actions:

1. Invest in mentorship: Connecting youth with mentors can significantly improve academic outcomes.

2. Technology literacy is essential: Equip students with digital skills to access new learning opportunities.

3. Extracurricular activities build leadership: Encourage involvement beyond the classroom to foster teamwork and responsibility.

4. Education reform requires collective pressure: Organize communities to advocate for equitable school funding.

5. Support vocational training: Promoting practical skills opens paths to meaningful careers.

6. Mental health support is non-negotiable: Integrate emotional well-being programs in educational spaces.

7. Community learning centers close gaps: Advocate for learning hubs offering tutoring and free resources.

8. Push for systemic changes: Engage in local school boards and policymaking to promote reforms.

9. Learning is lifelong: Encourage personal development at all stages of life.

10. Unity through education: Create intergenerational spaces where youth and elders share knowledge.

Chapter 2: Religion

Nurturing Faith and Empowering Futures: A Holistic Approach to Family Development

All Scripture is God-breathed and is useful for teaching, rebuking, correcting and training in righteousness. (2 Timothy 3:16 NIV)

Introduction

>Black religious institutions have long been pillars of strength within the African American community, providing spiritual guidance and serving as agents of social change. Rooted in a history of faith and activism, these institutions play a vital role in addressing the challenges of systemic racism, social instability, and inequality. This chapter explores the multifaceted role Black religious institutions have historically played, from promoting social justice to fostering economic empowerment and providing safe spaces for dialogue. We can appreciate these roles' continued significance in creating positive societal change.

Identification of Problems

- Inconsistent support for Black religious institutions despite their social and spiritual importance
- Difficulty maintaining 501(c)(3) tax-exempt status, hindering funding and donations

- The ongoing impact of systemic racism on Black religious institutions
- Lack of emotional and spiritual guidance in times of crisis
- Insufficient efforts in promoting social justice within communities
- Challenges in mobilizing communities for collective action
- Limited availability of safe spaces for open and honest discussions about racism
- Lack of focus on youth development and leadership training
- Economic instability within communities, limiting financial resources
- Difficulty fostering inclusiveness and embracing diversity within congregations

Identification of Solutions

- Strengthening support for Black religious institutions through advocacy and funding initiatives
- Ensuring compliance with IRS 501(c)(3) requirements to maintain tax-exempt status
- Addressing systemic racism's impact on religious institutions through educational programs
- Providing spiritual guidance and emotional support to communities in need
- Encouraging Black religious institutions to actively promote social justice and equality

- Facilitating community mobilization through workshops, rallies, and partnerships
- Offering safe spaces for discussions about racism and social justice within congregations
- Focusing on youth development through mentorship programs, leadership training, and education
- Supporting economic empowerment initiatives, such as financial literacy workshops and job training
- Promoting inclusivity within congregations, ensuring diverse voices are heard and valued

Benefits

1. Strengthened Religious Institutions: Increased support and funding for Black religious institutions will ensure they continue to play a vital role in promoting faith, social justice, and economic empowerment.
2. Enhanced Social Justice Efforts: By actively addressing systemic racism and inequality, Black religious institutions can drive progress in marginalized communities, promoting greater equality and unity.
3. Youth Leadership and Development: Mentorship programs and leadership training for youth will help develop future leaders within the church and the broader community, ensuring continued progress.

4. Community Mobilization: Safe spaces for discussions on social justice and racism and community engagement through workshops will foster collective action and a sense of belonging.
5. Economic Empowerment: Programs focused on financial literacy, job training, and economic growth will improve the financial well-being of community members, promoting long-term stability.

Conclusion

Black religious institutions are more than just places of worship; they are engines of social change and empowerment. The benefits they provide—from economic empowerment to social justice advocacy—are crucial to African American communities' continued growth and stability. By strengthening these institutions, we ensure they remain vital agents of change, fostering progress in all aspects of life.

Call to Action

Now is the time to support Black religious institutions as they continue to play a critical role in addressing systemic racism, fostering community empowerment, and promoting social justice. Please refer to the feedback checklist below to assess your understanding of these challenges and solutions. Scoring 8 out of 10 indicates a successful response to the issues discussed.

Instructions: Use this checklist to track your progress by marking "Yes" or "No" responses on paper or in your digital notes.

Feedback Checklist

1. Identified the key roles of Black religious institutions. Yes[] No[]
2. Recognized the importance of 501(c)(3) status for churches. Yes[] No[]
3. Understood the impact of systemic racism on Black religious institutions. Yes [ ] No [ ]
4. Addressed the significance of spiritual guidance and healing. Yes[] No[]
5. Highlighted the importance of promoting social justice. Yes[] No[]
6. Identified the role of community mobilization. Yes[] No[]
7. Recognized the need to provide safe spaces for dialogue. Yes[] No[]
8. Understood the role of Black religious institutions in youth development. Yes [ ] No [ ]
9. Recognize the importance of economic empowerment. Yes[] No[]
10. Provided actionable solutions for fostering inclusivity within congregations Yes [ ] No [ ]

Success Criteria: *8 out of 10 "Yes" responses = success.*

A.I. Reflections and Suggested Actions:
1. Faith-based initiatives create change: Partner religious institutions with community efforts.
2. Spiritual guidance promotes resilience: Offer support during social and personal crises.
3. Build interfaith coalitions: Collaboration between religions amplifies social justice efforts.
4. Religious spaces should foster dialogue: Create forums for open discussions on race and equity.
5. Invest in youth leadership programs: Prepare the next generation of faith-based leaders.
6. Advocate for inclusiveness: Promote diversity and acceptance within religious communities.
7. Support the financial health of churches: Strengthen the sustainability of faith institutions with proper funding.
8. Promote economic empowerment through faith: Teach financial literacy in congregational settings.

9. Engage communities through outreach: Use church spaces for education, health, and cultural activities.
10. Religion as a tool for activism: Use faith to inspire movements for systemic change.

Chapter 3: Leadership

Empowering Through Leadership: Creating Lasting Impact in Communities

When the righteous thrive, the people rejoice; when the wicked rule, the people groan. (Proverbs 29:2 NIV)

Introduction

> This chapter explores leadership through a combination of motivational and self-improvement messages with a strong call to action. It encourages individuals to embrace change, make hard choices, and cultivate sacrifice, vision, commitment, passion, and compassion. These attributes are essential for success and personal growth, particularly for those seeking to lead in their communities. Additionally, practical steps are provided for personal transformation over 30, 60, or 90 days, focusing on self-reliance, effective communication, emotional control, and sharing success. Leadership initiatives are discussed in the context of personal responsibility, continuous learning, and respect for others, particularly women. This section offers a comprehensive guide for those looking to lead effectively and foster community development.

Identification of Problems

- Lack of personal responsibility and failure to prioritize important aspects of life.
- Dependence on external forces (e.g.,

waiting for help from others) rather than self-reliance.
- Disrespect and exploitation of women within some communities.
- Neglect of continuous learning and self-improvement, even after formal education.
- Failure to support and uplift others in the community who are less fortunate.
- The inability to control behavior, emotions, and speech leads to negative consequences.
- Poor monetary management and lack of strategic planning in family and community settings.
- Failure to develop and implement a Prioritized Family Action Plan to address the community's personal, social, and economic problems.

Identification of Solutions

- Personal Responsibility: Individuals must learn to prioritize and make sacrifices, placing their welfare and families at the forefront.
- Self-Reliance: Focus on doing for oneself rather than expecting others (God, government, etc.) to provide. Embrace independent learning and self-sufficiency.
- Respect for Women: Treat women with dignity and respect, reject exploitation, and promote equal partnerships.
- Continuous Learning: Acknowledge that education is a lifelong process.

Pursue knowledge and skill development beyond formal schooling.
- Helping Others: Reach back and help others within the struggling community, fostering an environment of support and empowerment.
- Behavior Control: Learn to control one's actions, emotions, and speech to avoid negative outcomes and to be a model for others.
- Financial Discipline: Implement a Prioritized Family Action Plan to manage personal finances, addressing issues such as savings, budgeting, and long-term planning.
- Leadership in Action: Create a Family Action Plan for 30, 60, or 90 days, focusing on specific challenges in education, politics, religion, and economic development.

Benefits

1. Personal Growth: Developing personal responsibility and self-reliance will improve confidence, decision-making, and personal achievement.
2. Stronger Family Units: Respecting women and ensuring equality within family dynamics will strengthen familial relationships and create a positive home environment.

3. Lifelong Learning: Emphasizing continuous education will lead to personal and professional growth, creating a more knowledgeable and adaptable community.
4. Empowered Communities: Helping others will create a ripple effect, empowering those who receive help to uplift others, thus strengthening the entire community.
5. Better Financial Stability: Implementing a Family Action Plan will ensure better financial planning and security, reducing economic instability within the household and community.
6. Positive Role Models: Controlling behavior and emotions will set a positive example for younger generations, fostering a culture of respect and accountability.
7. Goal Achievement: Establishing and following a Prioritized Family Action Plan will enable families and communities to systematically address problems, making meaningful progress within a set time frame.
8. Community Leadership: Taking proactive steps in leadership initiatives will improve the overall well-being of the community, leading to greater unity, economic stability, and social progress.

Conclusion

> Leadership in Black communities must be anchored in personal responsibility, respect, and a commitment to continuous learning. By implementing the solutions outlined, individuals can transform their lives within 30, 60, or 90 days and extend this transformation to their families and communities. Empowerment, financial discipline, and positive leadership behaviors are critical to building a strong, self-reliant community that can overcome challenges and foster success. True leadership is about inspiring others to rise above their circumstances and work collectively for the betterment of all.

Call to Action

> Now is the time to embrace leadership and take charge of your personal and community growth. True leadership requires sacrifice, vision, and strong moral character, which includes commitment, passion, and compassion. Set clear goals, act purposefully, and lead by example in all areas of your life. Respect others, especially women, continuously seek self-improvement and help those less fortunate. By doing so, you will improve your own life and your family and community. Step up, act, and create lasting change—your leadership is needed now.

Instructions: Use this checklist to track your progress by marking "Yes" or "No" responses on paper or in your digital notes.

Feedback Checklist

1. Recognized the importance of personal responsibility. Yes[] No[]
2. Understood the need for self-reliance and independence. Yes[] No[]
3. Acknowledged the importance of respecting women in leadership. Yes[] No[]
4. Emphasized the value of continuous learning. Yes[] No[]
5. Identified the need to help others within the community. Yes[] No[]
6. Understood the importance of controlling behavior, emotions, and speech. Yes [ ] No [ ]
7. Highlighted the benefits of a Prioritized Family Action Plan. Yes [ ] No [ ]
8. Recognized the role of financial discipline in community success. Yes[] No[]
9. Emphasized setting goals and following through within 30, 60, or 90 days. Yes [ ] No [ ]
10. Identified the importance of leadership and mentorship in the community. Yes [ ] No [ ]

Success Criteria: 8 out of 10 "Yes" responses = success.

A.I. Reflections and Suggested Actions:

1. Leadership begins with personal responsibility: Take ownership of your goals and actions.
2. Self-reliance builds strength: Cultivate independence without waiting for external help.
3. Respect and equality are foundational: Treat all people, especially women, with dignity.
4. Continuous learning matters: Commit to lifelong self-improvement.
5. Mentorship builds future leaders: Guide others as you grow in your leadership journey.
6. Control emotions and behavior: Lead with discipline and set a positive example.
7. Financial planning is leadership: Implement strategic budgeting for family and community success.
8. Create action plans: Set specific, achievable goals for community progress within 30, 60, or 90 days.
9. Lead through service: Actively help others in your community.
10. Inspire by example: Be the change you wish to see.

Chapter 4: Economic Development

Faith and Financial Resilience: Building Prosperity Through Strategic Empowerment

Well then, you should have put my money on deposit with the bankers, so that when I returned I would have received it back with interest. (Matthew 25:27 NIV)

Introduction

>Faith plays a critical role in the success of family-focused entrepreneurs, guiding them through favorable and challenging times. This chapter explores how faith and wisdom can lead to success in small business ventures. Drawing from Biblical principles, it presents strategies that inspire perseverance, growth, and transformation in the financial success and stability journey.

Identification of Problems

- Lack of entrepreneurial guidance rooted in faith and wisdom
- Difficulty in adapting businesses to market changes
- Procrastination and failure to execute business plans
- Challenges in securing contracts and recovering from business losses
- Limited opportunities for lifelong learning and

personal development in business
- Lack of financial discipline and savings strategies
- Inadequate community support for Black-owned businesses
- Insufficient mentorship programs for young entrepreneurs
- Barriers to accessing capital and financial resources
- Economic instability within the Black community due to systemic inequalities

Identification of Solutions

- Emphasizing the importance of faith-based entrepreneurial guidance, drawing from Biblical teachings
- Encouraging business owners to embrace change and reinvent their businesses when necessary
- Promoting proactive planning and execution, eliminating procrastination and excuses
- Teaching resilience by learning from business losses and moving forward with courage
- Advocating for lifelong learning and self-improvement as essential for business success
- Implementing savings strategies such as setting aside a portion of earnings and investing wisely

- Supporting local Black-owned businesses through community engagement and collaboration
- Establishing mentorship programs where retired professionals can guide young entrepreneurs
- Providing access to capital through grants, loans, and investment opportunities
- Creating group economics and partnerships within the Black community to promote financial stability

Benefits

1. Entrepreneurial Success: Faith-based entrepreneurial guidance will equip small business owners with the resilience, wisdom, and perseverance needed for long-term success.
2. Adaptability: Encouraging businesses to embrace change and remain flexible will foster growth and sustainability in an evolving marketplace.
3. Financial Discipline: Promoting savings strategies and financial literacy will help entrepreneurs build wealth, maintain stability, and prepare for the future.
4. Community Support: Increased support for Black-owned businesses through local engagement will strengthen the economic foundation of the entire community.

5. Mentorship and Access to Capital: Mentorship programs and improved access to financial resources will empower young entrepreneurs, helping them overcome barriers to success.

Conclusion

Faith and wisdom are powerful tools in the pursuit of financial success. By integrating these principles with proactive planning and community support, entrepreneurs can build lasting businesses that contribute to their communities' economic growth and stability. Family businesses can thrive and testify to the power of faith-driven entrepreneurship through mentorship, financial discipline, and adaptability.

Call to Action

Now is the time to act. Entrepreneurs, community leaders, and families must embrace these strategies and build a solid foundation for economic growth. Please refer to the feedback checklist below to assess your understanding of these challenges and solutions. Scoring 8 out of 10 signifies a readiness to address these economic issues effectively.
Instructions: Use this checklist to track your progress by marking "Yes" or "No" responses on paper or in your digital notes.

Feedback Checklist

1. Recognized the role of faith in business success. Yes[] No[]
2. Understood the need for adapting businesses to market changes. Yes[] No[]
3. Identified the importance of executing business plans without procrastination. Yes[] No[]
4. Acknowledged the value of learning from business losses. Yes[] No[]
5. Recognized the need for lifelong learning and personal development in business. Yes[] No[]
6. Identified savings and investment strategies as crucial for financial stability. Yes[] No[]
7. Highlighted the importance of supporting local Black-owned businesses. Yes[] No[]
8. Understood the value of mentorship programs for young entrepreneurs. Yes[] No[]
9. Recognized the need for increased access to capital and financial resources. Yes[] No[]
10. I identified the role of group economics in promoting financial stability within the community. Yes [ ] No [ ]

Success Criteria: 8 out of 10 "Yes" responses = success.

A.I. Reflections and Suggested Actions:
1. Group economics strengthens communities: Foster partnerships and cooperative businesses.
2. Financial literacy is key: Promote budgeting, investing, and savings strategies.
3. Support Black-owned businesses: Engage in community buying and promote local entrepreneurs.
4. Entrepreneurship builds wealth: Equip individuals with business development tools.
5. Mentorship programs matter: Connect aspiring entrepreneurs with experienced mentors.
6. Access to capital is crucial: Advocate for policies supporting loans and grants for minority-owned businesses.
7. Embrace adaptability: Encourage businesses to pivot in response to market shifts.
8. Practice collective investment: Use community-based investment pools to fund new ventures.
9. Teach generational wealth planning: Prepare families to sustain financial growth across generations.
10. Link faith and finance: Use spiritual principles to guide ethical business practices.

Chapter 5: Politics
Leadership and Coalition Building: Paving the Way for Lasting Change

He changes times and seasons; he deposes kings and raises up others. He gives wisdom to the wise and knowledge to the discerning. (Daniel 2:21 NIV)

Introduction

"Who is ready to change? Creating opportunities now!" This powerful statement reflects individuals' need to step up and take charge of their lives and communities. Success, whether personal or political, requires sacrifice, vision, and difficult trade-offs. This chapter introduces the importance of leadership, emphasizing that true leaders possess character shaped by commitment, passion, and compassion. The following section outlines strategies for personal and community transformation, urging individuals to organize rather than criticize, develop clear goals, and push for progress in both personal and political spheres. This sets the stage for discussing political empowerment and coalition building within Black communities.

Identification of Problems

- Systemic racism continues to disenfranchise the Black community.

- Economic inequality persists due to historical discrimination.
- Black voters often face obstacles in accessing the policies they need.
- Political underrepresentation limits the power of the Black community in decision-making.
- The criminal justice system disproportionately impacts Black individuals.
- Limited access to quality education hinders upward mobility.
- Voter suppression tactics undermine Black political participation.
- Black communities lack sufficient influence in national politics.
- Integration weakened the sense of self-reliance within Black communities.
- Special interest groups control many elected officials, distancing them from the needs of the Black electorate.

Identification of Solutions

- Create independent, progressive political coalitions focused on addressing the unique needs of the Black community.
- Demand government accountability for laws and policies that perpetuate disparities.
- Engage in strategic voting to prioritize racial justice and economic equality.

- Push for policies that address systemic racism, such as housing reform and economic empowerment programs.
- Promote criminal justice reform to end over-policing and harsh sentencing for Black individuals.
- Expand access to high-quality education, emphasizing resources for underserved communities.
- Build coalitions with other marginalized communities to increase political influence.
- Empower Black youth to participate in politics through mentorship and education.
- Rebuild strong, self-sufficient Black communities through education, religion, and economic development.
- Monitor and hold politicians accountable to ensure they work for the people rather than special interests.

Benefits

1. Increased Political Power: Forming independent, progressive political coalitions will amplify the voice and influence of the Black community in decision-making processes at all levels of government.
2. Government Accountability: The community can push for policies that directly benefit marginalized groups by holding elected officials accountable for addressing disparities.

3. Racial Justice and Equality: Strategic voting and policy advocacy will help advance the cause of racial justice, ensuring that Black communities receive fair treatment in all aspects of life, including housing, education, and employment.
4. Criminal Justice Reform: Promoting reforms in the justice system will lead to fairer policing, sentencing, and treatment for Black individuals, reducing racial disparities.
5. Youth Political Engagement: Encouraging young people to become politically active will ensure the development of future leaders equipped to continue advocating for progress and equality.

Conclusion

Political empowerment is not just an option; it is a necessity for the Black community to overcome systemic barriers and inequalities. The Black community can build a more equitable society by forming coalitions, demanding accountability, and engaging in strategic voting. The benefits of coalition-building, youth engagement, and political reforms will have long-lasting effects, ensuring a future where the community thrives with greater influence and justice.

Call to Action

Now is the time to act. Build coalitions, demand accountability, and push for policies that promote equity and justice. Please refer to the feedback checklist below to assess your understanding of the issues and strategies discussed. Achieving a score of 8 out of 10 demonstrates a readiness to address Black communities' political challenges.

Instructions: Use this checklist to track your progress by marking "Yes" or "No" responses on paper or in your digital notes.

Feedback Checklist
1. Recognized the need for independent, progressive Black political coalitions.   Yes [ ] No [ ]
2. Understood the importance of government accountability for laws that perpetuate disparities.   Yes [ ] No [ ]
3. Identified the significance of strategic voting for racial justice and economic equality.   Yes [ ] No [ ]
4. Acknowledged the need for policies addressing systemic racism.   Yes [ ] No [ ]
5. Recognized the importance of criminal justice reform for Black communities.   Yes [ ] No [ ]
6. Understood the value of expanding access to quality education.   Yes [ ] No [ ]
7. Identified the role of coalition-building in increasing political influence.   Yes [ ] No [ ]

8. Highlighted the need for youth engagement in political processes.   Yes [ ] No [ ]
9. Recognized the importance of rebuilding self-sufficient Black communities.   Yes [ ] No [ ]
10. Understood the importance of holding politicians accountable.   Yes [ ] No [ ]

Success Criteria: 8 out of 10 "Yes" responses = success.

A.I. Reflections and Suggested Actions:

1. Coalition-building increases influence: Unite marginalized groups for greater political power.
2. Vote strategically: Support candidates and policies that align with the community's needs.
3. Demand accountability: Hold elected officials responsible for promises and policies.
4. Educate voters: Create voter education campaigns to increase participation.

5. Promote youth political engagement: Empower young people to join leadership roles.
6. Monitor policy impacts: Stay informed about legislation affecting the community.
7. Advocate for criminal justice reform: Push for laws that ensure fairness in the legal system.
8. Engage in local politics: Influence policies by participating in town halls and elections.
9. Support independent candidates: Back leaders who prioritize marginalized communities.
10. Encourage self-reliance: Promote community self-sufficiency alongside political engagement.

Chapter 6: Corrective Action Plan for Global Solutions

Implementing Strategic Steps to Unite, Innovate, and Drive Lasting Change.

In the same way, faith by itself, if it is not accompanied by action, is dead. (James 2:17 NIV)

Introduction

> This chapter outlines a structured 30, 60, and 90-day corrective action plan to address key problems affecting the Black community worldwide. The framework emphasizes individual and collective action, with clear timelines, leadership roles, and evaluation processes.

Identify a Problem

> Each corrective plan begins by identifying a significant global issue impacting the Black community. This includes educational disparities, economic marginalization, political disenfranchisement, and spiritual or leadership development access.
>
> - **Examples:** Limited access to quality education, insufficient financial literacy programs,

underrepresentation in leadership roles, or lack of mental health resources

Appoint a Program Problem Manager

Designate a leader responsible for overseeing the corrective process. This person acts as a central coordinator, ensuring that all aspects of the plan are implemented effectively.

- Key Role: The manager must collaborate across all five action areas: education and training, religion, leadership, economic development, and politics.

- Outcome: A consistent and focused effort driven by accountability.

Set Specific Goals

Each problem must have measurable goals to track progress. These objectives should align with local and global needs, ensuring scalable solutions.

- SMART Goals: Specific, Measurable, Achievable, Relevant, and Time-bound.

- Global Adaptation: Goals should reflect regional differences but contribute toward shared global outcomes.

- **Examples:** By Day 30, assess available educational programs; by Day 60, initiate pilot projects; by Day 90, evaluate outcomes and propose policy changes.

4. Provide a Checklist and Timeline (30, 60, 90 Days)

The 30, 60, and 90-day structure breaks the solution into manageable phases, ensuring continuous progress.

Day 30:

- Initial assessment of the problem.
- Identify stakeholders and resources.
- Draft a preliminary strategy.

Day 60:

- Implement early interventions or pilot solutions.
- Monitor ongoing activities, making mid-course corrections.

Day 90:

- Complete interventions and prepare a

final evaluation report.

- Present outcomes to stakeholders and community leaders.

- The timeline ensures accountability at every stage, providing structured opportunities to measure success or pivots, as necessary.

Appoint a 3-member Evaluation Team.

Select an independent review team responsible for evaluating the impact of the corrective action. This team ensures transparency and impartial feedback.

- Role of Evaluators:
    - Monitor progress and gather feedback.
    - Evaluate effectiveness in addressing root problems.
    - Prepare a final report with recommendations.
- Long-Term Vision: The evaluation team will also identify which aspects of the plan can be replicated or scaled for other communities worldwide.

Five Areas of Action

To create a comprehensive impact, problem-solving teams will operate across five interconnected areas:
1. Education and Training: Improve educational access and provide continuous learning opportunities, focusing on literacy, vocational training, and digital skills.
2. Religion and Spirituality: Promote unity through spiritual development, creating spaces for interfaith dialogue and collaboration within the global Black community.
3. Leadership: Develop leaders with a global perspective who understand local needs but work toward a shared vision for the future.
4. Economic Development: Build sustainable economic frameworks, including entrepreneurship, cooperative businesses, and investment in Black-owned enterprises.
5. Politics and Governance: Strengthen political engagement through education about civic rights, voting processes, and advocacy strategies.

A.I. Reflections and Suggested Actions:

1. Start small, think global: Local initiatives can inspire global movements.

2. Accountability ensures success: Use 30, 60, and 90-day timelines for progress tracking.

3. Collaboration multiplies impact: Work across sectors and communities for greater change.

4. Data-driven decisions are essential: Use research and feedback to shape interventions.

5. Set SMART goals: Ensure objectives are Specific, Measurable, Achievable, Relevant, and Time-bound.

6. Appoint dedicated leaders: Leadership roles ensure accountability and focus.

7. Evaluate regularly: Implement continuous assessments to refine strategies.

8. Create replicable models: Share successful initiatives across communities.

9. Engage youth in global solutions: Empower the next generation to lead globally.

10. Work toward long-term change: Focus on sustainable strategies that yield lasting results.

Appendix:

5-Year Plan for Regional Resort Development

This plan outlines a strategy to create six regional centers focused on conventions, meetings, retreats, and recreation.

These centers will feature hotels, golf courses, convention centers, and housing. Below is the financial breakdown and timeline to achieve this goal over the next five years.

Membership Contributions

- Total Members Contributing: 24,568,500
- Annual Contribution per Member under Disciple Principal: $12.00
- Total Annual Fund Contribution: $294,822,000.00
- Total Fund Over 5 Years: $1,474,110,000.00
- Adjusted for Inflation (5 Years): $1,565,250,037.78

Construction/Operational Costs and Timeline

- Base Cost per Regional Center: $250,000,000
- Total Cost Without Inflation: $1,500,000,000.00
- Total Cost With Inflation Adjustment: $1,617,102,471.08
- Estimated Years Needed for Completion: 6 years (1 center completed per year)
- Total Construction Jobs Created: 6,000
- Total Permanent Operational Jobs Created: 3,000
- Total Housing Units Needed: 600
- Total Operational Costs (5 Years): $64,684,098.84

This project is designed to leverage community stewardship funds to foster economic development. The six regional centers will serve as a hub for conventions, community events, and recreation, promoting tourism and local business growth.

The centers will be located in different regions of the United States, including the Northeast, Southeast, Northwest, Southwest, North Central, and South Central regions. Strategic construction over the five years ensures that funds are utilized efficiently, with an inflation adjustment factored into the overall project costs. By encouraging contributions from members and carefully managing the construction process, this project aims to promote sustainable growth and economic development across these regions.

Below is the timeline for the construction and operational phase of each center:

Financial Overview of the Total Members and Funds of The American Based Black Denominations

Contributions

- Total Members: 24,568,500

- Annual Fund Contribution: $294,822,000.00

- Total Fund Contribution (5 Years): $1,474,110,000.00

- Inflated Fund Contribution (5 Years): $1,565,250,037.78

- Total Cost (No Inflation): $1,500,000,000.00

- Total Cost (With Inflation): $1,617,102,471.08
- Years Needed for Completion: 6

Construction and Operational Timeline

Year 1
Center: Center 1
- Construction Jobs Created: 1,000
- Operational Jobs Created: 500
- Annual Operational Costs: $10,000,000

Year 2
Center: Center 2
- Construction Jobs Created: 1,000
- Operational Jobs Created: 500
- Annual Operational Costs: $10,300,000

Year 3
Center: Center 3
- Construction Jobs Created: 1,000
- Operational Jobs Created: 500
- Annual Operational Costs: $10,609,000

Year 4
Center: Center 4
- Construction Jobs Created: 1,000
- Operational Jobs Created: 500
- Annual Operational Costs: $10,927,270

Year 5
Center: Center 5
- Construction Jobs Created: 1,000
- Operational Jobs Created: 500
- Annual Operational Costs: $11,255,088

Year 6
Center: Center 6
- Construction Jobs Created: 1,000
- Operational Jobs Created: 500
- Annual Operational Costs: $11,592,741

Church Organizations

African Methodist Episcopal Church (AME)
- Year Founded: 1787
- Membership: 3.5 million
- Locations: U.S., Caribbean, Africa

African Methodist Episcopal Zion (AMEZ)
- Year Founded: Late 18th century
- Membership: 1.2 million
- Locations: U.S., Caribbean, Africa

Christian Methodist Episcopal Church (CME)
- Year Founded: 1870
- Membership: 800,000
- Locations: U.S., West Africa, Haiti, Jamaica

Church of God in Christ (COGIC)
- Year Founded: Early 20th century
- Membership: 5.5 million
- Locations: U.S.

Baptist Conventions (NBCA, NBC, PNBC)
- Year Founded: Various
- Membership: 13.5 million
- Locations: U.S., additional countries

United Methodist Church (UMC)
- Year Founded: 1784
- Membership: 12 million
- Locations: Primarily U.S.

Presbyterian Church (USA)
- Year Founded: 1807
- Membership: 65,000 Black members
- Locations: U.S., Africa, Southeast Asia

Sources of Funding and Importance of the 5-Year Resort Development Plan

The 5-Year Resort Development Plan aims to create six regional centers for conventions, meetings, retreats, and recreation to boost economic growth and community engagement. A critical component of the project's success will be sustainable funding through member stewardship and other sources. Below is an outline of the funding model and why this project is essential.

Primary Sources of Funding

1. Member Stewardship Contributions: Annual Contributions: Each member contributes $12.00 annually to the project.

   1. Projected 5-Year Total: With approximately 24.6 million members across multiple denominations, the total member contributions will yield $1.48 billion over five years (adjusted for inflation).

   2. Steady and Predictable Funding: This funding source ensures predictable cash flow, allowing for phased project development without relying heavily on loans or external grants.

2. Government and Community Grants:
    1. State and Federal Grants: Programs that support economic development and tourism in underserved communities will be tapped to supplement construction costs.
    2. Municipal Incentives: Many cities offer tax incentives and grants to attract projects that promote tourism, increase employment, and enhance community engagement.
3. Corporate Sponsorships and Partnerships:
    1. Collaboration with hospitality companies, golf course developers, and convention center operators will help offset costs through strategic sponsorships.
    2. Naming rights or in-kind contributions (e.g., equipment, marketing) will reduce development expenses.
4. Loans and Bonds (if necessary):

Low-interest municipal loans or community bonds may cover short-term funding gaps if needed. However, the goal is to minimize debt and ensure that contributions remain the primary funding source.

Importance of the Project

This initiative represents a critical investment in the future of African American religious organizations and their communities by fostering economic independence and sustainable development. Below are some key benefits:

1. Economic Development and Job Creation:
   1. The regional resorts will generate construction, hospitality, tourism, and event management jobs.
   2. They will promote small business development, providing opportunities for local entrepreneurs to thrive.
2. Community Engagement and Cultural Preservation:
   1. These centers will offer venues for conventions, meetings, and retreats, reinforcing connections within the denominations and with the broader community.

2. They will serve as hubs for cultural events, preserving African American heritage while attracting visitors from across the country.

3. Tourism and Revenue Generation:

   1. Hosting large conventions and retreats will attract tourists, generating additional revenue through lodging, dining, and leisure activities.

   2. A sustainable flow of tourism income will contribute to long-term financial stability for the centers and the surrounding areas.

4. Promoting Self-Reliance and Stewardship:

   1. The reliance on member contributions reinforces the importance of collective stewardship, empowering the community to take ownership of its development.

   2. This model reduces dependency on external funding, fostering financial self-sufficiency over time.

5. Strengthening Regional Networks:
   1. Placing one center in each U.S. region ensures this initiative's impact is widespread and inclusive.
   2. The centers will enhance collaboration between regional and national organizations, leading to stronger networks and shared resources.

This plan offers more than just physical infrastructure—it is a blueprint for economic and social empowerment. By pooling resources and creating opportunities for engagement and development, these resorts will serve as pillars of growth, benefiting the churches and uplifting surrounding communities.

In conclusion, the 5-Year Regional Resort Development Plan embodies the principles of unity, stewardship, and economic self-reliance. It leverages the collective strength of historically African American denominations to build lasting legacies for future generations.

Banking Establishment Plan: Regional Centers and Main Bank

Introduction

This Banking Establishment Plan lays the financial foundation for the 5-Year Regional Resort Development Plan, ensuring responsible management of resources and promoting economic self-reliance. With a network of regional financial centers connected to a main bank, the plan offers a blueprint for sustainable growth, fostering community unity, power, and prosperity. This comprehensive strategy includes a timeline, key roles, governance structure, sources of funding, and regulatory requirements to ensure sustainable development.

1. Structure and Key Functions Main Bank (Headquarters)
- Location: Atlanta, Georgia (chosen for its role as a financial hub with strong connections to Black businesses).
- Functions:
    - Centralized management of contributions, grants, and partnerships.

- Oversee regulatory compliance at the federal and state levels.
- Administer loan programs, investments, and sponsorships.
- Provide financial oversight to regional financial centers.

Six Regional Financial Centers

- Locations:
    1. Northeast (New York)
    2. Southeast (Atlanta)
    3. Northwest (Seattle)
    4. Southwest (Dallas)
    5. North Central (Chicago)
    6. South Central (Houston)
- Functions:
    - Manage local construction funds, payroll, and operational expenses.
    - Coordinate with municipalities to secure grants, incentives, and partnerships.
    - Offer financial literacy programs to empower churches and community members.

2. Sources of Money

  1. Membership Contributions:

     - Each member contributes $12 annually.

     - Total Funds Raised Over 5 Years: $1.48 billion (adjusted for inflation).

  2. Government and Community Grants:

     - Leverage federal and state economic development grants.

     - Apply for municipal incentives, such as tax breaks and tourism grants.

  3. Corporate Sponsorships and Partnerships:

     - Collaborate with hospitality companies, golf course developers, and convention center operators.

     - Generate additional revenue through naming rights and in-kind contributions.

  4. Loans and Bonds:

     - Secure low-interest municipal loans or community bonds to cover temporary funding gaps.

3. Timeline and Key Milestones Year 1:

Year 2:

- Open the second financial center in the Northeast region.
- Roll out community loan programs for housing and small businesses.
- Continue construction of the second resort center.

Year 3:

- Launch the third financial center in the Southwest region.
- Partner with hospitality companies for sponsorships.
- Begin the third resort center construction project.

Year 4:

- Establish the fourth financial center in the Northwest region.
- Introduce community grants and bonds for entrepreneurs.
- Launch construction of the fourth resort center.

Year 5:
- Complete the fifth financial center in the North Central region.
- Expand small business loans and tourism partnerships.
- Open the fifth resort center.

Year 6:
- Finalize the sixth financial center in the South Central region.
- Integrate mobile banking services.
- Complete construction of the sixth and final resort center.

4. Key Personnel and Governance Structure

CEO Qualifications
- At least 15 years of experience in banking, finance, or non-profit leadership.
- Proven success in managing large-scale projects and ensuring regulatory compliance.
- Expertise in community banking with strong ties to African American development initiatives.

Example Candidate:

- A former executive from a credit union like One United Bank.

Key Executive Roles

- **CFO:** Oversees financial operations and regulatory compliance.
- **COO:** Manages operations, staffing, and construction funds.
- **CRO:** Monitors risk management and internal audits.
- **CTO:** Leads digital banking services and cybersecurity.

Board of Directors

- Composition:
  Representatives from participating denominations (AME, COGIC, CME, Baptist conventions) and law, finance, and economic development experts.
- Role:
  Provide strategic guidance, ensure accountability, and approve major investments and partnerships.

5. Regulatory Requirements and Compliance

1. Bank Charter:
   - Apply for a federal or state charter to operate legally.
   - Submit financial statements, business plans, and personnel information.

2. FDIC Registration:
   - Insure customer deposits up to $250,000 per depositor.

3. Community Reinvestment Act (CRA):
   - Ensure credit access to communities, especially underserved areas.

4. Anti-Money Laundering (AML) and Know Your Customer (KYC) Compliance:
   - Implement robust fraud prevention protocols.

6. State Compliance:
   - Follow tax, labor, and banking regulations in each state.

Impact and Vision

The Banking Establishment Plan plays a pivotal role in the success of the 5-Year Regional Resort Development Plan. A network of regional financial centers connected to a main bank ensures transparency, accountability, and efficient resource management. Each center aligns with resort construction timelines, enabling phased development, job creation, and sustainable operations.
Member contributions provide predictable cash flow, minimizing reliance on debt. Partnerships with local governments, hospitality companies, and small businesses diversify revenue streams.

Loan programs foster entrepreneurship and provide affordable housing, promoting economic growth. Financial literacy programs empower community members to become stewards of their financial future. The Board of Directors ensures decisions align with community needs, maintaining trust and transparency. Adhering to regulatory guidelines like the CRA and FDIC build credibility and protect deposits, ensuring financial stability.

Conclusion

This Banking Establishment Plan ensures the seamless integration of fiscal management with the development of regional resort centers. By promoting economic empowerment, community stewardship, and sustainable development, this initiative fosters a framework for long-term growth. Through collective ownership and strategic partnerships, the network of regional financial centers and the main bank will create lasting opportunities for prosperity and unity across the African American faith community.

With the right leadership and community involvement, this plan offers a sustainable legacy of economic growth, cultural preservation, and self-reliance for future generations.

Acknowledgment of A.I. Contribution

Portions of this document, including the organization, structure, and formatting, were developed with the assistance of artificial intelligence using OpenAI's ChatGPT. A.I. contributed to streamlining the content, generating ideas, and refining the presentation to ensure clarity, coherence, and ease of use for readers. Final editorial decisions and responsibility for the material rest with the author.

> ***I have set an example that you should do as I have done for you. John 13:15 NIV***

About the Author

Dr. Eldridge Henderson is a visionary leader and advocate for the Black community, with over 35 years of experience in business operations management, focusing on leadership, organizational development, and community empowerment. He has dedicated his career to addressing systemic barriers faced by Black Americans in politics, education, and economic development.

Raised in a family that values faith and service, Dr. Henderson has consistently used his expertise to uplift communities and inspire future generations. His educational journey began at the Utica Institute in Mississippi, followed by Jackson State University, and culminated at Atlanta University, where he gained valuable perspectives that inform his leadership today.

This book represents the culmination of his research and commitment to social justice, offering a roadmap to a more equitable and empowered Black America. In addition to his writing, Dr. Henderson hosts the long-running radio show *Organize, Don't Criticize* on WMPR, 90.1 FM in Jackson, MS, providing practical advice on organization and personal development. He also conducts workshops and seminars based on the six chapters of this book, empowering aspiring entrepreneurs and making a significant impact in the community.

Acknowledgments

I extend my heartfelt gratitude to Tennie White for her invaluable assistance over the past two years on my book, *Organize, Don't Criticize*. This project has been a true labor of love, and Tennie's unwavering support has made all the difference.

Tennie, your enthusiasm for this journey has inspired me, and I have cherished every moment of our collaboration. Thank you for believing in this vision and being integral to its realization. Your contributions have enriched this work in countless ways, and I am deeply grateful for your partnership.

What Readers Are Saying About "Organize, Don't Criticize"

The following quotes reflect the impact and importance of *Organize, Don't Criticize*, as shared by readers from various backgrounds. Their words highlight the transformative power of the book and its role in shaping the future of the Black community.

"Organize Don't Criticize is the global survival bible for Black people."
— *E. K.*

"Those who read and act on the solutions referenced in *Organize, Don't Criticize* will change their lives in one generation."
— *L. F.*

"The Black race had never had a theoretical perspective that defined a strategy for determining its destiny from birth to death until the publication of *Organize, Don't Criticize*. This book is a beacon of hope for the future of the Black community."
— *P. B.*

"Organize, Don't Criticize" is not an illusion of inclusion. This book prioritizes corrective action for the Black diaspora worldwide."
— *R. Y.*

Made in the USA
Columbia, SC
09 May 2025